Landscapes

Elizabeth Nonweiler

raintree

canyon

heath

mangroves

coastline

tea farm

pastoral land

soil and rocks on Mars

volcanic mountain

fir tree forest

sand dunes of the desert

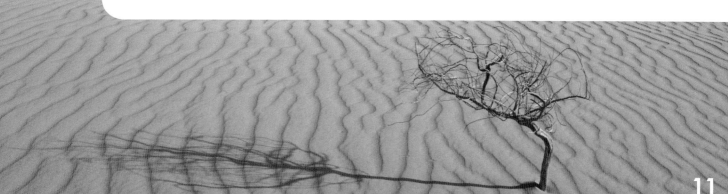

limestone pavement

urban landscape

Interesting facts about the pictures

page 2: A **canyon** is a deep narrow passage between tall cliffs, often with a river running through it. This is the Grand Canyon in the United States. In places it is nearly 2 kilometres deep.

page 3: A **heath** is open land with low bushes and shrubs. This heath has purple heather and yellow gorse growing on it. Some heaths were once forests, but people cut down the trees.

page 4: **Mangroves** are groups of trees that grow in mud and salty water near the sea. They have massive roots that get covered as the tide rises and uncovered again as it falls.

page 5: A **coastline** is the place where land meets sea. Coastlines can have sandy beaches, pebble beaches, mudflats, lagoons, salt marshes, rocks or caves. This one in Australia has tall cliffs.

page 6: A **tea farm** grows the best tea when it is in a warm, rainy place, high above the sea. The tea bushes are planted in rows and cut at waist height, so that people can pick the leaves easily.

page 7: **Pastoral land** is land used by farmers for their animals to graze (eat grass). Cattle, sheep, goats, deer, llamas, horses or pigs can graze on pastoral land in fields called pastures.

page 8: The **soil and rocks on Mars** are a reddish colour because they are partly iron oxide (rust). No people have been to Mars, so this photo was taken from a vehicle with a camera but no driver.

page 9: **Volcanic mountains** are formed when an explosion underground sends out enormous amounts of melted rock and ash that pile up into a mountain. This one is still smoking.

page 10: **Fir tree forests** are often on cold mountains. Fir trees stay green all year, so people use them as Christmas trees to show that there is life, even in the middle of winter.

page 11: A **desert** is a place where it hardly ever rains, so almost nothing lives there. It is very hot in the day and very cold at night. The wind blows desert sand into hills called **sand dunes**.

page 12: **Limestone pavements** are where glaciers (sheets of ice) came and went thousands of year ago, taking away the top of rocks, leaving cracks. They look like man-made pavements.

page 13: An **urban landscape** is one with lots of roads and buildings. This is a city in China called Fuzhou (pronounced like "Foojoe"). More than 2 million people live there.

Letter-sound correspondences

Level 2 books cover the following letter-sound correspondences.
Letter-sound correspondences highlighted in **green** can be found in this book.

ant	**b**ig	**c**at	**d**og	**e**gg	fish	**g**et	**h**ot	it
jet	**k**ey	**l**et	**m**an	**n**ut	o**ff**	**p**an	**qu**een	run
sun	tap	**u**p	**v**an	**w**et	bo**x**	**y**es	**z**oo	
du**ck**	fi**sh**	**ch**ips	si**ng**	**th**in **th**is	k**ee**p	l**oo**k m**oo**n	**ar**t	c**or**n

s**ay**	b**oy**	r**ai**n	**oi**l	b**oa**t	**ea**t	p**ie**	h**igh**
m**a**k**e**	th**e**s**e**	l**i**k**e**	n**o**t**e**	fl**u**t**e** t**u**b**e**	**ou**t	s**aw**	**au**thor
h**er**	b**ir**d	t**ur**n	**air**port	fl**ew** st**ew**	bl**ue** c**ue**	**ph**one	**wh**en